Little Boy Jonny and the Wild and Free Day

Adina Crump

Alex Patrick

This is a work of fiction. Names, characters, places, and incidents either are the product of the author's imagination or are used fictitiously. Any resemblance to actual persons, living or dead, events, or locales is entirely coincidental.

Copyright © 2023 by Adina Crump

All rights reserved. No part of this book may be reproduced or used in any manner without written permission of the copyright owner except for the use of quotations in a book review.

First print edition 2023

Cover and Illustrations © Alex Patrick, 2023, licenced exclusively by The Bright Agency: thebrightagency.com

Book design by Veronica Scott

ISBN 979-8-9876799-0-6 (hardcover)
ISBN 979-8-987-6799-1-3 (ebook)

For Asher,

My incredibly sweet and wonderfully wild little boy

Little boy Jonny woke up one day.
Before he got dressed and went out to play,
He decided he wanted to be WILD AND FREE
And do things *a little bit differently.*

This little boy Jonny had not a care.
He couldn't be bothered with UNDERWEAR.
His mother said, "Honey, come put these on please!"
"NO!" cried the boy. "I need to be FREE!
I want to feel the crisp cool breeze!"

"Look, Mommy, look! In the forest are bears.
THEY don't have any underwear.
If their bum is not frolicking FREE,
They can't scritch and scratch on the perfect tree!"

"How different am I? What's different with me?
I'm like the bears, WILD AND FREE!
Bare bum for me—that's how I will be!"

When little boy Jonny had the chance,
He couldn't, just *wouldn't*, put on his PANTS.
His mother said, "Dear, please put these on now."
"NO!" cried the boy. "No way, no how!
I have to be FREE to jump up and down."

"Look, Mommy, look! How the kangaroos leap!
If *THEY* wore pants, it would be a defeat.
They must bounce and bound, hip and hop,
With no pants on *them*, making them stop."

"How different am I? What's different with me?
I'm like the kangaroos, WILD AND FREE!
No pants for me—that's how I will be!"

This naughty boy had quite the knack of ripping the SHIRT right off of his back. His father said, "Come put your shirt back on please!"

"NO!" cried the boy. "I'm out climbing trees! I can't have a shirt hindering me!"

"Look, Daddy, look! Way up high are the monkeys.
If THEY wore shirts, they'd surely be grumpy.
They couldn't stretch and swing from the trees,
Or pick their bunch of bananas with ease."

"How different am I? What's different with me?
I'm like the monkeys, WILD AND FREE!
No shirt for me—that's how I will be!"

Little boy Jonny didn't want to wear SHOES. When he was asked, he flatly refused.

His mother said, "Please put your shoes on. Let's go!"

"NO!" cried the boy. "I *like* mud in my toes, slopping and sloshing around to and fro."

"Look, Mommy, look! On the farm there are pigs.
THEY don't wear shoes in the mud when they dig.
How could they stomp and romp and play
With silly old shoes ruining their day?"

"How different am I? What's different with me?
I'm like the pigs, WILD AND FREE!
No shoes for me—that's how I will be!"

Jonny started to whine and mope
At the thought of having to put on a COAT.
His father said, "Son, come please put this on!"
"NO!" cried the boy. "This coat feels all wrong!
It's too big, too little, too short, too long!"

"Look, Daddy, look! On the mountain are goats.
THEY never would ever put on a coat.
How could they climb from cliff to cliff
With a zippered up coat, making them stiff?"

"How different am I? What's different with me?
I'm like the goats, WILD AND FREE!
No coat for me—that's how I will be!"

Now little boy Jonny was quite in a TIZZY, TWIRLING around and getting real dizzy.

"Mommy, Daddy, why is it so?

Pigs are fine with no shoes on their toes.

Goats have no coats. No complaint do they utter.

Bears have no underwear.
They do not shudder.

Without their shirts,
the monkeys all thrive.

The kangaroos jump
and feel so alive."

"How can I lose
With no shirt or shoes?
Watch me dance
With no coat or pants!
If my bum is bare,
I do not care!
Animals do it...
ANIMALS DO IT!

They are not clueless...
There's something to it!

Clothes are *useless* and *foolish*
And frankly quite *prudish*!
AND I RESOLUTELY WON'T DO IT!"

His parents looked at each other and sighed.
They knowingly said, "He might as well try."
"Alright little one, out you can go
Without a shirt, Without a coat,
Without your pants, Without your shoes,
Without underwear—just do as you choose."

Without his shoes, he stubbed his toe.

He climbed a tree with no pants or shirt
And got a few scratches that really did hurt.

"Oh no! I see! How silly of me!
I realize bare-skinned I cannot be.
Some animals have fur. They need not have clothes.
And some have hooves that protect their toes.

I need clothes to cover my skin
From scratches and stones, from mud and from wind.
I cannot go out in the world so bare.
I understand now, and these clothes I shall wear."

Mommy spoke softly, as she bandaged his knee.
"These rules keep you safe and protect you, you see?
But if **WILD AND FREE** is how you will be,
Just think how to do it differently."

Jonny grinned and turned to his mom and dad,
For he had a thought that made his heart glad.
He shouted with triumphant glee,
"In the BATH, I can truly be FREE!"

"No underwear, no need for a coat.
Just cover me up with bubbly soap!
In the water I have no use
For pants or shirt or silly old shoes!

Here I will stay from morning till noon
Until I turn into a wrinkly prune."

When it was night, AT LAST he came out.

He put on pajamas with *not even* a pout.

He snuggled up with his covers so tight
And kissed his mom and dad goodnight.
There in his bed he stayed snuggly warm
Until daylight broke the next morn.

And before little boy Jonny went out to play,
He happily put on his clothes for the day.

THE END

ABOUT THE AUTHOR:

Adina grew up reading the humorous poems of Shel Silverstein and Jack Prelutsky. They stayed with her and through the years inspired her to put pen to paper, capture meaningful moments in life, and turn them into rhymes. In 2020 Adina and her husband had their first baby, a wild and mischievous but deliciously sweet little boy. His daily antics have brought loads of laughs and provide the inspiration for this story, which Adina hopes will entertain and amuse its readers as well.

ABOUT THE Illustrator:

Alex Patrick was born in the Kentish town of Dartford in the South-East of England and has been drawing for as long as he can remember.

His lifelong love for cartoons, picture books and comics has shaped him into the passionate children's illustrator he is today. Alex loves creating original characters - he brings an element of fun and humour to each of his illustrations and is often found laughing to himself as he draws.

Printed in the USA
CPSIA information can be obtained
at www.ICGtesting.com
LVRC081117130224
771729LV00012B/472